I0158274

Energy Vampires for Young Adults:

Managing Stress & Negative Thoughts in Your
Personal & School Life

Tara C. Dale

Copyright © 2018 by Tara Dale

All rights reserved. No part of this book may be reproduced in any form or by an electronic or mechanical means, including information storage and retrieval systems. It cannot be copied for public or private use, except for the "fair use" or as brief quotations used in articles and reviews without prior written consent of the publisher.

ISBN 978-0-578-52742-0 (paperback)

Dedication Page

This book is dedicated to all of my children: my two biological children and the 1,600 temporarily adopted children who I taught throughout my many years in the classroom. May all of you realize that you make choices every day, which puts you in control of your life. My advice? Make good choices so that more good things happen to you than bad things. I love you all! I most especially love and adore my sweet, wonderful, kind, and generous Joshua and Samantha.

A personal thank you to Aubrey Alcala for helping me edit the book, vetting it through your young adult eyes. Your insight was priceless. Your comments were sincere. Your suggestions were useful, introspective, and so very thoughtful! I love you, girl! Thank you for your honesty and willingness to open your heart. I am a better person because I know you. May you find the courage to continue to dream as you create your life's adventure.

Table of Contents

Forward

I first met "Mrs. Dale" through my daughter Summer, as her science teacher in middle school. Summer told me great things about Mrs. Dale: what a great teacher she was, and how much she loved learning and teaching. She was my daughter's favorite teacher. After meeting with Tara at a Parent Teacher conference, I gave her a copy of my book, <u>Energy Vampires: Managing your Stress in Your Personal and Professional Life</u> and after reading it, she said she could relate to it personally and professionally. She also mentioned that her students deal with their own kind of Energy Vampires. Her views about the concepts, especially the "Concept of 3," were right in tune with the message I was writing for adults. I knew she was perfect for writing the young adult version of Energy Vampires.

Tara has the personal and professional experience working with middle, high school, and college students to cover the same concepts in my book, but using their language. By putting it into workbook format, Tara's book is a great guide to help young adults recognize and deal with the Energy Vampires in their personal and, especially, school lives. Her book is perfect for use in secondary classes by teachers as a personal growth and development opportunity to help open up important discussions about Energy Vampires, which may include bullying.

It was a pleasure to work with my friend, Tara, aka "Mrs. Dale" and I believe you, your child, and your students will greatly benefit from the information in her book. Enjoy your journey of self-discovery and make it the best! Remember, the "Choice is yours!"

Dr. Steve Ornelas

Preface

"You are enrolled in a full-time informal school called Life. Each day in this school you will have the opportunity to learn lessons. You may like the lessons or think them irrelevant and stupid."

- Cherie Carter-Scott, international author and entrepreneur

How did I come up with this title and the content of this book? Good question. My friend, Dr. Steve Ornelas, wrote the book Energy Vampires for adults. He asked that I write the same book but for young adults, including teenagers. If you are familiar with his book, you will notice that I have duplicated his format and even began with the same quote.

In his preface, Dr. Ornelas explains that life is school. You may disagree. You may think of school as a building where teachers stand in front of the classroom, giving you a bunch of information so that you can pass a test. I agree with you - life is not that type of school. However, school is more than that. School is an opportunity to experience new people and new situations. School teaches you about yourself and your family. Life teaches you this too. Life is a set of opportunities and experiences that teach you about your family, your friends, and most importantly, YOU!

Think of a time when you were not at school but instead were hanging out with friends. Maybe you were at the mall searching for a new boy/girlfriend or looking for that perfect pair of shoes. Maybe you were playing video games or swimming at a pool party. It does not matter. Just think of any time you were with friends.

My guess is that if you thought long and hard about that situation, you would realize that you learned something about yourself. Maybe you learned that although you found someone cute, you did not have the courage to approach them and introduce yourself. Maybe you learned that although you found that perfect pair of shoes, you could not steal them because you have morals and standards. Maybe you learned that you are a gracious winner when you won every video game you played that day. Or maybe you learned that you can swim faster than all of your friends.

Regardless of your memory, at that specific time in your life, you were just living life but there life was, teaching you something.

What does this have to do with vampires? Another good question! Dr. Ornelas explains that Energy Vampires are "people, situations, or things in your life that drain you of your energy." He goes on to tell his readers that it is important to identify the Energy Vampires in your life so that you can control the amount of the energy they suck from you.

My goal for you, dear reader, is to walk away from this book feeling like you have more control of your life. Life should not be what happens to you. Life should be how you react to the things that happen to you.

Charles R. Swindoll, an international Christian pastor, tells his congregation, "I am convinced that life is 10% what happens to me and 90% how I react to it." Once you realize that you have control over 90% of your life, you will find that you have more energy and time to focus on the things you truly love doing. You will be happier and you will be emotionally and mentally healthier.

What should your goal be as you read this book? Yet, a third good question. You are full of them today! Your goal is to think while you read. I know that sounds silly. Let me explain what I mean.

Have you ever read something and then afterwards realized that you had no idea what you just read? I do this all the time. It means that I'm reading the words but I'm not thinking about them. When this happens, I cannot tell you what I just read and I certainly cannot tell you the meaning of what I just read.

Your goal is to think about the words as you read them and then to reread sentences that you do not understand. If you promise to think while you are reading, I promise that you will be happier and healthier when you are done with this book.

You Have Control Over Your Life!

*"I discovered I always have choices and
sometimes it's only a choice of attitude."*

- Judith M. Knowlton, recovering alcoholic, now famous author

As a teacher, I know that when students know the purpose of a lesson, they are more likely to learn and understand the lesson. Therefore, I want you to know the two purposes of this book so you are more likely to understand its messages.

The first purpose is for you to identify the people, events, and situations in your life that drain you of your energy. These Energy Vampires can make you miserable by giving you low self-esteem; removing control of your own life; and/or negatively affecting relationships with your parents, siblings, and friends.

The second purpose of this book is to provide you with skills that will help you to manage your Energy Vampires. There is no point of identifying your Energy Vampires if you cannot manage the amount of energy they suck from you.

Now let's talk about the purpose of this chapter. Why should you read it? Let me tell you. This chapter is going to convince you that you have control over your life. According to Swindoll, you have 90% control of your life. That is a lot of control!

I've worked with middle and high school students for more than a decade and after many conversations with them, I found it is not unusual for them to believe Swindoll is wrong. I am going to challenge your thinking and prove to you that YOU do have control over your life. Your parents, teachers, bosses, etc. do not control you.

Many young adults feel as though they are controlled by laws and rules that were created by family, teachers, their boss, their city, and/or friends. That is simply not true. You have choices. You are not being physically forced to do anything.

You make approximately 1,000 decisions every day. Some decisions happen automatically so you do not realize you are making them. For example, when you decide to brush your teeth in the morning, you do it automatically. You probably do not debate this decision by listing all of the reasons you should brush your teeth and all of the reasons you should not brush your teeth and then use that information to make a final decision. Brushing your teeth is automatic for someone your age so it is an automatic decision and you do not even realize you are making it. It is still a decision you make daily because you do have the freedom to not brush your teeth.

Some decisions are more memorable and require internal debate, such as, "No, I will not smoke marijuana." If you have been confronted with the choice to do drugs, you probably very aware that you were making a choice. There was probably some internal struggle that you experienced before you made the decision. It probably was not an automatic decision but instead was a decision that you knew you were making at the time you made it.

Let's do a quick activity. If you do not have a pencil, go get one. I will wait for you.

Welcome back! You are going to complete two sentences. Be honest with yourself and do not try to be silly because then the exercise will be meaningless for you.

The first sentence starts with "I can't...." Finish it. What is something in your life that you are <u>not allowed to do</u>? As an example, one of my students by the name of MacKenzie wrote, "I can't date until I'm 16-years-old."

1. I can't...

The second sentence starts with "I have to..." Finish it. What is something in your life that <u>you have to do</u>? As an example, one of my college friends named Alyx wrote, "I have to attend school every day."

2. I have to...

Now, in the first sentence, scratch out the word "can't" and replace it with "choose not to" and in the second sentence, scratch out the word "have" and replace it with "choose".

Now read your new sentences. MacKenzie's new sentence read as "I choose not to date until I'm 16-years-old." And Alyx's new sentence read as "I choose to attend school every day."

Do you agree with your new sentences? MacKenzie did not agree with her new sentence about not being able to date because she explained that her mom would get mad and ground her for dating before she was 16-years-old, which was the house rule. However, Alyx agreed with her sentence because no one was forcing her to go to her college classes. Her professors do not take attendance so no one would know if she was present or absent.

But I argue that MacKenzie and Alyx's sentences are correct. Yes, it is true that if MacKenzie went on a date then she would get into trouble <u>but that would be MacKenzie's choice</u>. Follow the flow chart below and see if you can find out why MacKenzie

chooses to follow her mom's rule about not dating.

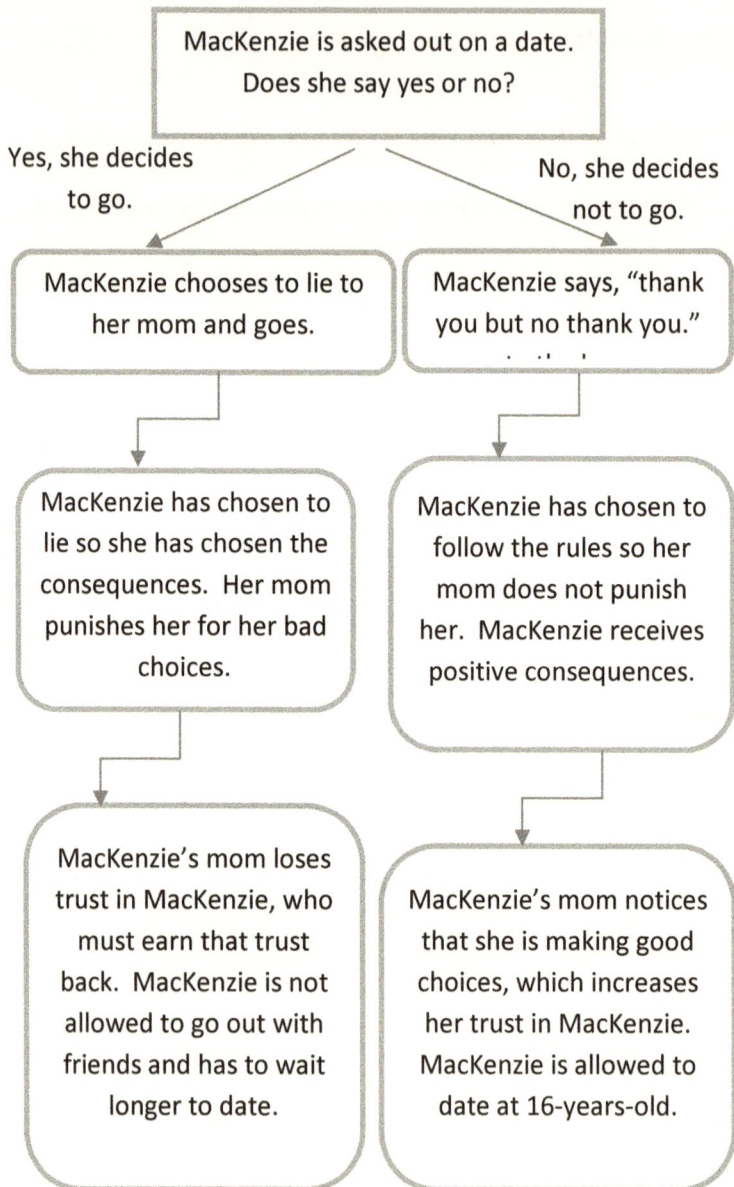

MacKenzie is asked out on a date.
Does she say yes or no?

Yes, she decides to go.

No, she decides not to go.

MacKenzie chooses to lie to her mom and goes.

MacKenzie says, "thank you but no thank you."

MacKenzie has chosen to lie so she has chosen the consequences. Her mom punishes her for her bad choices.

MacKenzie has chosen to follow the rules so her mom does not punish her. MacKenzie receives positive consequences.

MacKenzie's mom loses trust in MacKenzie, who must earn that trust back. MacKenzie is not allowed to go out with friends and has to wait longer to date.

MacKenzie's mom notices that she is making good choices, which increases her trust in MacKenzie. MacKenzie is allowed to date at 16-years-old.

Why do you believe that MacKenzie chooses to follow her mom's rule? Write your answer here:

I think MacKenzie chooses to wait until she is 16-years-old to date because she values her mom's trust. She realizes that when she chooses to follow her mom's rules, she is building her mom's trust and that eventually it will pay off when she turns 16-years-old. After all, her mom could delay her dating until she is 17-years-old (or later) if she does not trust MacKenzie.

List three things that MacKenzie has control over.

1.

2.

3.

As a teacher, I feel obligated to provide you with an answer key

But you need to realize that there are many correct answers so

you may have something written on page 15 that I did not think

of and that is OK. Here are three things MacKenzie definitely

has control over:

1. MacKenzie controls how she behaves toward her mom.

2. MacKenzie controls if she lies to her mom.

3. MacKenzie controls if she follows her mom's rules.

That is a lot of control MacKenzie has over her own life!

Let me give you another example. This is a personal

example. After my son turned 16-years-old, he bought himself

a car. When he made good choices, such as doing his

homework and not lying, then he told his friends that his mom

was "chill," meaning that I was relaxed and allowed him to go to

the movies and hang out with his friends. But when he made

poor choices, then I was no longer "chill" because I would no

longer allow him to have a social life until after he rebuilt his trust with me. My son had control over our relationship. When he made good choices, I behaved in one way and when he made poor choices, I behaved in a different way. But it was my son who set the tone for our relationship as he was growing from a boy to a man. He was the one in control.

What about Alyx? Alyx lived on campus, not with her parents. But she still had to manage her relationships with her teachers and more importantly, with herself.

Alyx CHOOSES to attend her classes because she does NOT HAVE TO go to class. Let us pretend as though her professors did take attendance and were aware that she was ditching class. It is still Alyx's CHOICE to go to class. Students can ditch but then they are also CHOOSING the consequences. Alyx is CHOOSING positive consequences over negative consequences. She is CHOOSING to do well in school by attending her classes because one day she wants to go to medical school. She is making CHOICES that help her avoid negative consequences such as low grades, losing her scholarships, and not meeting the requirements for medical school. It is Alyx's CHOICE, which means Alyx has control over her school life.

You make hundreds, if not thousands, of choices every day. You choose to attend school or you choose not to attend school. You choose to do your homework or you choose not to do your homework. You choose to do your chores or you choose not to do your chores. You choose to go to work or you choose not to go to work. You choose to follow rules and laws or you choose not to follow rules and laws.

You make positive choices, such as attending school, going to work, and following the law, because you want to avoid negative consequences. The bottom line is that you have a lot of control that you may not even realize. And you make many decisions every day than you probably realize.

What is your opinion? Return to your new sentences on page 12. Do you agree or disagree with your new sentences that say "I choose not to..." and "I choose to..."?

What choices do you make every day? Can you easily document ten daily choices? Try it in the spaces below. If you have difficulty, think about chores, jobs, or how you interact with family members and friends. What rules are created by teachers, parents, or the law that you choose to follow?

1.

2.

3.

4.

5.

6.

7.

8.

9.

10.

Look at the ten things you listed above and think about what positive consequences would occur if you followed them and what negative consequences would occur if you did not follow them. For example, one of the things on my list is that I choose to be respectful to all of my students, even if they are not respectful to me.

If I choose to respect my students then the positive consequence is that I will have a good relationship with them and their parents. If I choose to disrespect my students then I will have negative consequences. My students and their parents will not respect me or trust me. They will report me to my principal and if my actions are bad enough, I could lose my job. Now this can get ugly really quickly because these negative consequences cause other negative consequences, which affect me and the people who love me. If I lose my job, then my family loses my income. I will no longer receive my paycheck so we will have to get rid of some expenses. The first thing to go is family fun, such as my son's basketball games and my daughter's gymnastics meets. We would not be able to go on vacation and or go out to eat. There would be no money for these fun things until I got another job, which would be difficult because other schools would find out that I was a disrespectful teacher and would not want to hire me.

I choose to respect my students every day for two reasons. First, it's the right thing to do – we should treat everyone with respect. Also because I do not want negative consequences to happen to my family and me.

Before we move on to the next chapter, did you achieve the purpose of this chapter? Do you understand that you have control over your life about 90% of the time? Do you believe that you make choices all day long, even if you are not aware of them?

If you do not agree with me, try doing the first activity once again with the "can" and "can't" sentences on page 12. What are things that you do not feel you have control over? Then change your sentences to "choose to" and "choose not to". Do you agree or disagree with your new sentences?

Are you really controlled or are you making decisions in order to avoid negative consequences such as low grades, punishments, or jail time? As Dr. Ornelas always says, "The choice is yours!"

"You have brains in your head. You have feet in your shoes. You can steer yourself any direction you choose."
- Dr. Seuss

<u>"The Concept of 3"</u>

"The world that we live in is the one that we create. We create our world with every thought that we think, with every word that we speak, and with every action that we take."

- LeVar Burton, American actor

Just as in the last chapter, let us begin with the purpose of this chapter. Why read this chapter? This chapter is going to explain "The Concept of 3," which is a term coined by Dr. Ornelas. We established that you control 90% of your life by the choices you make. There are three types of choices you make daily, which make up "The Concept of 3." Once you understand The Concept of 3, you can identify additional ways to control your life. Here are the three types of choices:

1. How you think about you and the world

2. How you feel about you and the world

3. How you react in the world

How You Think About You and the World

Do you believe you have control over how you think about the people around you? I am embarrassed to admit that I did not realize I had control over my thoughts until I was about 34-years-old. I had a friend who we will call Tracy. When I was 34, it dawned on me that every time someone mentioned my friend Tracy, I immediately felt disappointment. Tracy had disappointed me multiple times, throughout our relationship.

I always felt disappointment because Tracy continually disappointed me. Then a friend gave me good advice. She suggested that I lower my expectations of Tracy. I needed to CHOOSE a different thought about my friend Tracy.

I tried this technique the next time that Tracy promised me something. I CHOSE to think differently about her. Instead of thinking that Tracy would follow through with her promise, I CHOSE to think that she would not keep her promise. Two weeks later Tracy failed at her promise. It was the first time I did not feel angry or disappointed towards Tracy and it was because I never thought she was going to fulfill her promise in the first place. By changing my thoughts (my expectations), I took control of our relationship. I no longer felt angry or sad when I interacted with Tracy because I no longer allowed her to have that control over me. I now have the control. The choice was mine and it is YOURS!

You too have control about how you think about people and situations in your life. You CHOOSE how to think about people and you CHOOSE how to think about things that happen to you.

My friend, Jill, comes to mind immediately. Jill's family lost their home during the flooding caused by Hurricane Katrina. They were homeless so they moved to Arizona to live with Jill's uncle. Jill CHOSE to think of her situation as an opportunity. She thought of moving to Arizona as an opportunity to live in a new place and make new friends.

Jill arrived in Arizona sad that she had lost her old home but CHOSE to be optimistic about her new home. Her positive thoughts helped her to make wonderful friends and achieve excellent grades. Jill CHOSE to think positively and see her situation as an opportunity. The choice was hers and it is YOURS!

Directions: Identify one person or situation in your life that is negativity affecting you right now. Describe the person or situation that negatively affects you:

Write down what negative thoughts you currently have about this person or situation:

Describe how you can change your thoughts so that this person or situation affects you less negatively:

How You Feel About You and the World

Many people believe there are good and bad feelings. Here is a list of how *most* people would categorize feelings:

Good Feelings	Bad Feelings
Happiness	Sadness
Excitement	Envy
Anticipation	Jealousy
Joy	Angry

However, this categorization is incorrect. Feelings are neither good nor bad but instead just are! As the saying goes, "it is what it is."

It is difficult to choose your feelings and maybe we should not. Dr. Ornelas says, "...suppressing thoughts and...feelings is unhealthy." He continues to say, "Feelings give us the flavor of life. They are the things that remind us that we are ALIVE! We should never feel afraid of feeling emotions." I completely agree with Dr. Ornelas. Your feelings are important and they are yours.

Life coach, Cindy Holbrook said, "You shouldn't ever let anyone tell you how you should feel about any given circumstance." If someone surprises me with a gift of peanut butter candies, of course I am going to be happy because I love peanut butter. It is not good or bad to be happy in this situation. It just is.

If someone lies to me, of course, I am going to be angry and if someone dies, of course I am going to be sad. It is not bad to have these feelings. They just are. What is important is what you do with these feelings.

We have established that emotions are not good and are not bad. And we acknowledge that they are difficult to choose.

However, you can choose how to feel about yourself 100% of the time. Eleanor Roosevelt, wife of the United States' 32nd President, once said, "No one can make you feel inferior without your consent." I love this quote! Mrs. Roosevelt understood that you have ownership over how you feel about yourself.

When my friend, Jules, was in high school she was teased relentlessly for how she dressed. Despite the bullying that Jules experienced, she chose to feel good about herself. She chose to focus on the good things in her life such as her kid brother and her love of soccer. Jules chose to feel happy about the woman she was. The choice to feel good was Jules' and it is YOURS!

Directions: Write three positive words that describe you.

1.

2.

3.

Think about the three positive words you just wrote down. How would you respond if someone came up to you right now and said that those three words are not a good

description of you? Document your response here:

How did you respond? Did you give them control by

choosing to believe them? Or did you take control and choose

not to believe them? Remember that the choice is YOURS!

If you gave them control and chose to believe them,

challenge yourself. Write down examples that prove that the

three words you documented on page 29 are representative of

who you are. I left some space for you to document your ideas:

How You React in the World

What about having control over your behavior? You have considerable control over how you think and feel but you have complete control over how you behave and react. Return to the table on page 27 that lists good and bad feelings.

As I stated, these feelings are neither good nor bad. It is OK to feel any of those feelings. But how you react to those feelings are 100% completely in your control.

You cannot say, "my sister made me do it" when you hit her or "she pushed all my buttons and that's why I slapped her." It was OK that you were angry with her but it was not OK that you hit her.

Although you did not have a choice about being angry, you did have a choice about how you behaved when you were angry. Remember that feelings are neither good nor bad but just are. It is what you do with your feelings that matters.

What can you choose to do when you experience a "bad" feeling? First, write down a feeling that most people consider "bad", such as anger, jealousy, or hatred: _____

Now fill out the two columns, brainstorming positive and negative behaviors you can choose when you experience that "bad" feeling. For example, if experience the "bad" feeling of anger because your sister is an Energy Vampire, a positive behavior is to hit a pillow and a negative behavior is to hit her.

Positive Behaviors	Negative Behaviors

When you choose a positive behavior, you will experience positive consequences but when you choose a negative behavior, you will experience negative consequences.

You have a choice. You can choose behaviors in the Positive Behavior column or the Negative Behavior column. No one can make you behave in a way that you do not want to behave. The choice is YOURS!

Additionally, people learn how to treat you based on how you behave. Wow! That is deep. Let me explain.

As I mentioned before, life is a school. You are the student and the teacher at the same time. You teach people how to treat you by having control over your thoughts, feelings, and behavior. Let me give you another personal example. When my daughter turned 13-years-old, I explained to her that if she make good choices then I would be more likely to trust her, which means I would be more likely to answer "yes" to questions such as, "can I go to the mall with my friends?" or "can I see a movie Saturday night?"

However, if she made bad choices then I would not be able to trust her and I would be more likely to tell her "no" when she asked me to go to the mall or the movies.

Both of my children are consistently teaching me how to treat them. If they choose good behaviors, then they teach me to treat them with trust but if they choose bad behaviors, then they teach me to treat them with mistrust.

My children are the teachers and I am the student. I react to how they behave. My children are in control of our relationship just like you are in control of your relationships. Your behavior teaches people how to treat you. You probably have more control over your life than you originally thought!

You are a student but you are also a teacher. Do you find that surprising? You learn things outside of the classroom every day. For example, you have learned how to behave in a movie theatre and how that is different from how you behave in a library. You learned that in a movie theatre you must be quiet; however, it is acceptable to scream when something scary jumps out at you and it is acceptable to laugh out loud when the story has something funny in it. In a library, you must be quiet all of the time, even when the story becomes scary or funny.

Outside of the classroom, you can also learn how to treat people. As an example, when a friend is angry with you, you learn what makes them angry so you can avoid it in the future. When I was in college, my roommate was angry that I had a party while she was at work and I did not clean up before she got home. She was right. I should have cleaned up the mess before I went to bed so that she did not have to clean when she arrived home. She sat me down and explained how my choices affected her. I learned that I needed to clean up before going to bed. I learned how to treat my roommate with respect because she taught me how to do so. YOU also are a teacher every day. You teach people how to treat you. Think about that for a moment. I'll wait.

Document a recent behavior that you exhibited that taught someone else how to treat you. Did you positively reward a choice that someone else made and it inspired them to continue making good choices? Did you give someone negative

feedback (like my roommate did when I didn't clean up after

the party) and it motivated them to change their choices? Place

your thoughts here:

As a mom, I teach my own two children every day how

to treat me. I do not need to do it through anger. One day I

punished my son for making a bad choice and he told me that

he hated me. My response? I hugged him. I know that he did

not really hate me. Instead, he was actually mad at himself that

he had made a bad decision and was being punished. But, it

was easier to be mad at me than to admit that he was wrong.

As I hugged him, I whispered in his ear, "I love you. I

love you no matter what you do. I don't always like you but I

always love you. And you feel the same about me. You always

love me but you don't always like me. You don't hate me. You are just angry." I was teaching my son that he should not say that he hates me because the fact is that he does not hate me. I was teaching my son that it is OK to not like someone all the time because, let's face it, that is life.

I was also teaching my son that although he may feel as though he hates me, he needs to realize the origin of those feelings. It was not my fault, after all, that he made a bad choice. That was his fault. He needed to own his bad decision, realize that he disappointed himself, and not be angry with me.

That day, I taught my son how to treat me. Since this occurred, he has never once told me that he hates me. And it was a good reminder for me: although I was angry with him for making a bad choice, I still loved him dearly. I chose my behavior that day. I chose to respond with a hug and instead of more yelling and more punishing.

You control how you behave when you interact with people. The choice is YOURS!

In this chapter, we discussed the "The Concept of 3", which consists of these three choices:

1. How you think about you and the world

2. How you feel about you and the world

3. How you react in the world

You might not always have control over how you think and feel but you always have control over how you behave and how you react to your thoughts and feelings. Antoine de Saint-Exupery, French author of <u>The Little Prince</u> said, "The meaning of things lies not in the things themselves but in our attitude towards them." The choice is YOURS!

Identify Your Energy Vampires and Plan Your Reaction

The purpose of this chapter is to help you identify your Energy Vampires and give you skills for how to react to them.

Energy Vampires are people who drain you of your energy. After you hang out with them, you feel weak and/or tired. These people can be friends, people at work, boyfriends or girlfriends, or family members. For example, if you have friends who consistently pressure you to do things that you do not want to do, these friends may be Energy Vampires. It is exhausting to continually tell your friends "no" when they want you to do something that you do not want to do.

When I was in high school I dated a boy who wanted me to see rated R movies but at the time, I was not allowed to see these movies. He told me to tell my parents that we were seeing a different movie that was rated PG, but I hated lying to my parents because they always caught me and I always got in trouble.

This boyfriend was an Energy Vampire because he made me choose between him and my parents' rules. It was a stressful relationship to be a part of because he consistently put me in these types of situations. I hated having to choose between making him happy and following my parents' rules so I finally chose not to date him anymore and kicked him to the curb.

Identify Your Energy Vampires

It can be difficult to identify who your Energy Vampires are because sometimes an Energy Vampire is someone you love and/or respect. Without knowing it, you may be making excuses for their behavior.

Here is an exercise you can do to identify your Energy Vampires. In order for this exercise to be successful, you have to be honest with yourself. Feel free to take some time to think about this, even if it requires a few days to complete it.

On the next page, fill out the concentric circles by first putting yourself in the middle circle. Then add the people you live with or spend the most time with, in the next circle. Use

the next ring for those people you see sometimes and continue

until you get to the most outer ring, which will include people

you very rarely spend time with.

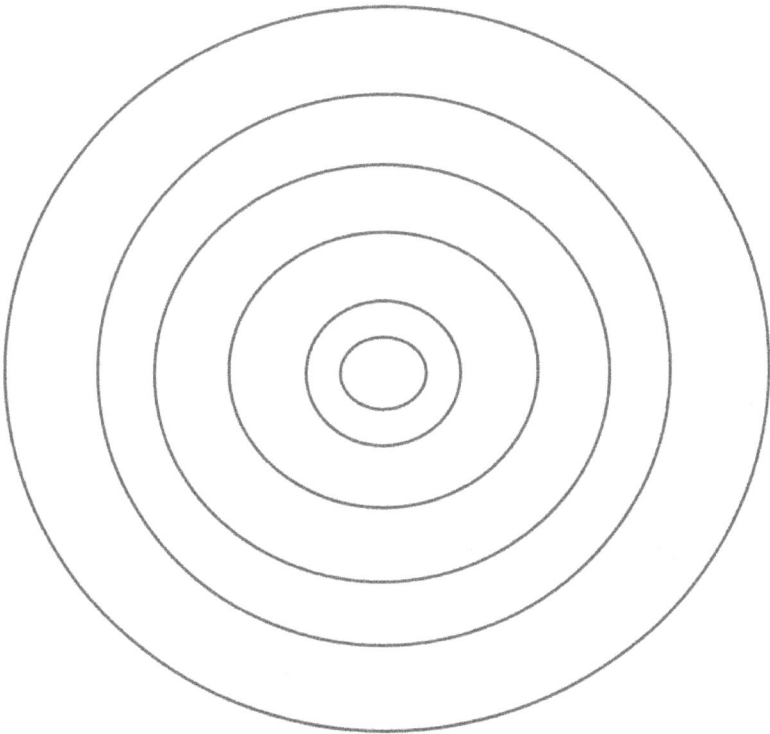

Now that you have everyone written in the circles, place

a negative sign (-) next to those people who bring negative

energy to your life and place a positive sign (+) next to those people who bring positive energy to your life. Some of your people may have both positive and negative signs, which is okay, but ultimately you need to decide if they are more positive or more negative. The people with negative signs are Energy Vampires and there are specific things you can do to manage how much energy they suck from your life.

Plan Your Reaction

How will you react to your Energy Vampires the next time you see them? How will you gain some control? First, realize that you have control. For example, when you are around these people, you have a lot of control over how you feel and think and you have 100% of control over how you react.

Before you meet up with them, try calming yourself by doing some breathing exercises or counting. Take a deep breath in through your nose while counting to five, hold your breath for six seconds, and then slowly breathe out of your mouth for seven seconds. Do this a few times until you feel relaxed, calmed, and in control of your emotions.

Remind yourself of "The Concept of 3," which states that you have control over how you think, feel, and react. You have control over what you will say to them, how you will react to their behaviors and attitudes, and sometimes you also have control over how much time you spend with them.

If you are forced to hang out with your Energy Vampires, such as a family member or a coworker, try to think differently about the situation so that you feel and react differently.

Abraham Lincoln said, "We can complain because rose bushes have thorns, or rejoice because thorn bushes have roses." If you can find something positive about your situation, such as "Yes, I have to hang out with my cousin but at least he is a good artist and can teach me how to draw," then you will be more likely to engage in a positively-controlled situation instead of something that is negative and leaves you drained of your energy. The choice is YOURS!

This leads me to my next question. Are you your own Energy Vampire? You need to be honest with yourself when you answer these next questions.

1. Do you like to be the victim?

2. Do you retell stories about terrible events in your life? Do you share these stories with others?

3. Do you think about and replay frustrating experiences in your head? Is it difficult to let go and move on?

It requires energy to play the role of a victim, retell stories of horrible events in your life, and constantly think about frustrating experiences. Doing these things will drain you, leaving you tired, sad, frustrated, and/or angry. Choose to learn how to let go so that you do not relive negative experiences again in your head. You choose how to think, feel, and react. Choose to be your own best friend. The choice is YOURS!

The purpose of this chapter was to identify your Energy Vampires and provide you with a plan for how to control the amount of energy they suck from you. If you do not feel like you accomplished this, go back and read the chapter again, identifying different choices you can make when dealing with your vampires.

<u>Document Your Plan</u>

Who is one Energy Vampire in your life? Write their name here:

Document how this person currently drains you of energy:

Now document one specific thing you will do differently when you are with this person:

Remember, the choice is YOURS!

If your life was made into a movie, what genre would you want it to be: drama, comedy, adventure, romance? Is it that way now? If not, what are some changes that you can make so that you have the life you want? Who would have a smaller role in your movie? Who would have a larger role? How each scene ends is up to YOU! The choice is YOURS! Use this space to organize your ideas and thoughts:

Islands of Stability

The purpose of this chapter is to give you tools you can use when life gets rough. Dr. Ornelas uses the analogy of life being like the ocean. Sometimes life is calm and fun but sometimes it has its storms and turbulence. What calm islands can you visit during the storms? When life is rough, what can you do to ride out the storm?

First, identify your storms, which could be many different things. One of my dear friends has a storm with her health. She has been ill for over a year now and still does not know what is wrong with her. She struggles every day with a constant throbbing pain in her neck and a tingly feeling in her fingers.

In addition to poor health, other examples of storms include failing grades, getting in trouble with the law, losing someone you love, and arguing with parents. Additional storms consist of feeling insecure about yourself, having too much pride, or being fearful of things. What are two of your storms? Document them here:

1.

2.

The first thing you have to know is that storms will happen. Bad things happen. They happen to bad people and they happen to good people.

Bad things are unavoidable (they are the 10% of your life that you cannot control) but you do have a choice about how to react when they occur (and you can control 100% of your reaction).

Jake Canfield and Kent Healy, two recognized authors, stated, "You must take personal responsibility. You cannot change the circumstances, the seasons, or the wind, but you can change yourself."

When the storms hit (when bad things happen to you), you need to have islands of stability. Your islands can be friends, parents, church leaders, coworkers, and teachers. In the previous chapter you filled out concentric circles, identifying the people in your life who are positive influences. These are possible islands of stability. Your islands of stability can also be a process that reduces stress such as exercising, writing in a journal or diary, throwing a football, snuggling with a beloved pet, or going to the park. Document who or what your top four stability islands are:

1.

2.

3.

4.

The other thing to consider is what to do if you are your own Energy Vampire. How can you change your thinking? What can you do instead of replaying, retelling, and reliving negative experiences? Document your ideas here:

Bad things will happen to everyone and there is no way to prevent them all. Storms occur and we have no control over them. However, we can prepare for them; after all, people get insurance so they can recover more easily after a storm passes.

You should prepare for your personal storms by making a plan. Heck, you are preparing right now by reading this book! That is a great step in the right direction! You are creating a plan by identifying your islands of stability before the storm hits. Pat yourself on the back for a job well done. The choice is yours and you have CHOSEN well!

The Last Chapter: Let's Put it all Together!

First Most Important Idea:

YOU HAVE CONTROL!
YOU CONTROL YOU!

You teach others how to treat you because you are always the teacher and the student. Life is school and you play both roles. You control most of how you think and feel and you control all of your behaviors. The choice is YOURS!

Second Most Important Idea:

IDENTIFY AND PLAN FOR YOUR ENERGY VAMPIRES.

Your Energy Vampires are the people that drain your energy. You feel tired or sad after you hang out with them. You can change how much energy they suck from you by changing your relationship with them. You can spend less time with them or change your focus when you are with them. How will you change how you think, feel, and react? The choice is YOURS!

Third Most Important Idea:

WHO AND WHAT ARE YOUR ISLANDS OF STABILITY?

When your ocean gets stormy, and it will, how will you cope? Who can you turn to when the waters get choppy and what can you do to relieve the stress that comes with your storms? You have 100% control over your reaction to these storms and it is best to have a plan before they hit. The choice is YOURS!

I will leave you with one last quote. "The only person responsible for the quality of your life is You. If you want to gain the respect of others and have more fun, you must take full responsibility for all you do...no blaming anything/anyone else." Jack Canfield and Kent Healy stated this in their book titled <u>The Success Principles for Teens: How to get from where you are to where you want to be.</u> The choice is YOURS!

About the Author

Tara Dale is a National Board Certified teacher. Mrs. Dale has a Bachelor's of Science degree in Psychology and another in Biology from Arizona State University. She also has a Master's degree in Secondary Education. Her mission in the classroom is to give life-long tools to her students so they may achieve all of their dreams. She focuses on thinking critically, problem solving creatively, and communicating effectively. In 2014, she was a finalist for Arizona State Teacher of the Year. Mrs. Dale is married to a fantastic man and has two wonderful children, who are her true successes in life.

About the Graphic Artist

Clay Farrow has been a graphic artist since 2000, working in both print and digital media. He lives with his wife Terri and their two ill-behaved dogs in Phoenix, Arizona. Mr. Farrow designed the front cover and created the logo for iNTENTIONAL SCHOLAR, LLC.

Recommended Reading

Jack Canfield and Kent Healy's "The Success Principles for Teens:
How to get from where you are to where you want to be."
(2008). Health Communications. Deerfield Beach, Florida.

Steve Ornelas's "Energy Vampires: Managing stress & negative
thoughts in your personal & professional life" would be a great
read for your parents/guardians. It's available at
www.lulu.com.

Sources

Burton, LeVar. Quote found at
http://www.gravityteen.com/think/Think.cfm?start=31.

Canfield, Jack and Kent Healy. The Success Principles for Teens:
How to get from where you are to where you want to be.
(2008). Health Communications. Deerfield Beach, Florida.

Carter-Scott, Cherie. Negaholics: How to overcome negativity
and turn your life around. (1989). Ballantine Wellspring.
www.drchierie.com.

Holbrook, Cindy. "What are Feelings?" 2013. Found on
December 26, 2013 at http://cindysense.com/what-are-
feelings.

Knowlton, Judith M. Quote found at
http://www.quotelady.com/subjects/choices.html.

Lincoln, Abraham. Quote found at
http://www.goodreads.com/quotes/67318-we-can-complain-
because-rose-bushes-have-thorns-or-rejoice.

Ornelas, Steve. Energy Vampires: Managing stress & negative
thoughts in your personal & professional life. (2007). GabSum
Productions, LLC. Phoenix, Arizona.

Roosevelt, Eleanor. Quote found at
http://www.brainyquote.com/quotes/quotes/e/eleanorroo161
321.html.

de Saint-Exupery, Antoine. Quote found at http://www.quotes-
positive.com/by/antoine-de-saint- exupery/.

Suess, Theodor. <u>Oh, the Places You'll Go!</u> (1990). Random House. New York, New York.

Swindoll, Charles R. Quote found at http://www.goodreads.com/author/quotes/5139. Charles_R_Swindoll.

www.ingramcontent.com/pod-product-compliance
Lightning Source LLC
Chambersburg PA
CBHW021919040426
42448CB00007B/822